TABLE OF CONTENTS

T0052479

HAVE HUMANS IMPACTED EARTH?

Ever since humans developed agriculture and built cities, they have impacted Earth in some way. It's estimated that 80 percent of Earth's land surface has been affected by human activities. Not only have people impacted Earth's land, but they have also impacted its **atmosphere**, **biosphere**, and **hydrosphere**.

The development and expansion of cities has displaced animals and eliminated their habitats.

atmosphere—the mixture of gases that surrounds Earth

biosphere—the part of Earth in which life can exist

hydrosphere—the part of Earth including bodies of water and water vapor in the atmosphere

Fact Finders®

HUMANS AND OUR PLANET

HUMAN ENVIRONMENTAL IMPACT

How We Affect Earth

by Ava Sawyer

CAPSTONE PRESS
a capstone imprint

Fact Finders Books are published by Capstone Press,
1710 Roe Crest Drive, North Mankato, Minnesota 56003
www.mycapstone.com

Library of Congress Cataloging-in-Publication Data
Names: Sawyer, Ava, author.
Title: Human environmental impact : how we affect Earth / by Ava Sawyer.
Description: North Mankato, Minnesota : Capstone Press, [2017] | Series: Fact finders. Humans and our planet | Audience: Ages 8–10. | Audience: Grades 4 to 6. | Includes bibliographical references and index.
Identifiers: LCCN 2017015796| ISBN 9781515771968 (library binding) | ISBN 9781515772101 (paperback) | ISBN 9781515772149 (ebook (pdf))
Subjects: LCSH: Human ecology—Juvenile literature. | Nature—Effect of human beings on—Juvenile literature. | Conservation of natural resources—Juvenile literature.
Classification: LCC GF48 .S285 2017 | DDC 304.2—dc23
LC record available at https://lccn.loc.gov/2017015796

Editorial Credits
Editor: Nikki Potts
Designer: Philippa Jenkins
Media Researcher: Jo Miller
Production Specialist: Kathy McColley

Photo Credits
Newscom: MCT/Maschletto, 8, UIG Universal Images Group/Encyclopaedia Britannica, 23; Shutterstock: Aerovista Luchfotografie, 20, airphoto.gr, 14, Arnain, 10, Asia Images, 24, BlueRingMedia, 21, Christopher Halloran, 12, Delpixel, 27, Diyana Dimitrova, 17, Egorov Igor, 26, Fouad A. Saad, 18, gallimaufry, 6, Gubin Yury, 7, javarman, 19, Kristo Robert, 11, Modfos, 5, Pix One, 15, Praethip Docekalova, 16, Rawpixel.com, throughout (background), Rich Carey, 9, Sergei Butorin, 4, Sinisha Karich, 25, Wollertz, 13, Zeljko Radojko, 22, zstock, cover

Some human activities have been positive for the environment. However, many results from human activities have been negative. Humans heavily rely on **natural resources**. They plow up natural vegetation and chop down forests. They send pollution into the air and dump chemicals into water resources. People may not realize how their actions can affect the environment.

natural resource—something in nature that is useful to people, such as coal and trees

CHAPTER 2

HUMAN IMPACTS

GARBAGE DISPOSAL

Garbage is a major human-caused problem. Landfills are huge garbage dumps that take over large areas of Earth's land. Some of the materials in these dumps take hundreds or thousands of years to **decompose** and break down. Objects such as plastics never completely decompose. Some thrown-out materials contain toxic, which means poisonous, chemicals. When those chemicals leak into the land, they pollute both the soil and the groundwater.

Garbage piles up in a countryside open landfill.

decompose—to rot or decay

A gigantic hill of garbage is placed near Moscow, Russia.

Landfills are also a problem because of methane gas. When materials like food, tree branches, and plants are covered up in a landfill, they break down in an **anaerobic** way. This causes the formation of methane gas, which is a **greenhouse gas**. It traps 21 times more heat in the atmosphere than carbon dioxide does.

anaerobic—not using oxygen

greenhouse gas—gases in a planet's atmosphere that trap heat energy from the sun

Garbage isn't only dumped on land. It is also dumped in the ocean — whether on purpose or by accident. Much of the garbage that ends up in the ocean is made up of plastics. Sunlight breaks down plastics into smaller pieces. However, the pieces don't disappear altogether. Garbage floats along ocean currents and then gathers together in big patches. One of the world's most famous patches is called the Great Pacific Garbage Patch. It's located in the Pacific Ocean between Japan and California. There are actually two distinct patches. One is between Japan and Hawaii. The other is between Hawaii and California.

The Great Pacific Garbage Patch is estimated to be twice the size of Texas.

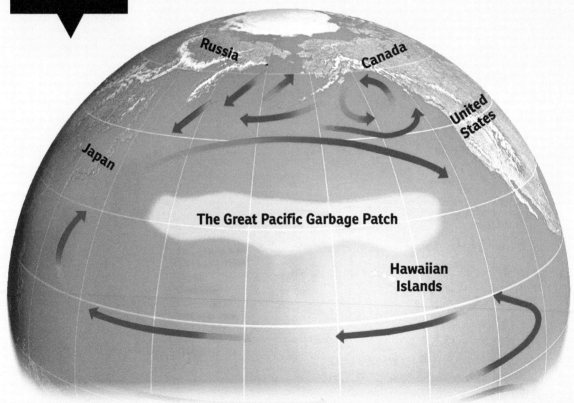

Russia

Canada

United States

Japan

The Great Pacific Garbage Patch

Hawaiian Islands

A small portion of Earth's garbage floats on the top of the ocean. The rest of the pieces — four billion or more — sink to the deep sea. Some of this garbage includes large objects such as water bottles, electronics, toys, and toothbrushes. They float across the oceans from beaches around the world. Sometimes they are thrown off ships in the ocean.

Garbage Patches

Garbage patches are found in every single ocean and sea around the world. Experts estimate that there are 5.25 trillion pieces of plastic in the oceans. Some of the garbage is very small — about the size of grains of rice. The sun has already broken those pieces down into smaller particles. Plastic in the ocean is extremely dangerous for animals that live there. They get tangled in it and mistake it for food. The presence of plastics can destroy marine life.

Plastic and metal containers sit on the ocean floor among sea life.

FOREST DEPLETION

Forests are hugely important to the survival of our planet. They keep the carbon dioxide and oxygen in our atmosphere balanced. The tropical rain forests are of particular importance. These are often called Earth's "lungs" because they provide the atmosphere with so much oxygen.

Forests are cut down for many reasons, but it takes many years for them to fully grow back to what they once were.

For many years the wood from forests has been used as a fuel and a building material. Sometimes forests are cleared to make room for farmland or to raise cattle. These forests are **renewable** because they can be replanted. However, people are using up this resource more quickly than it can be replaced. The trees in some forests take hundreds of years to fully grow.

renewable—restored or replaced by natural processes

CHAPTER 3
NONRENEWABLE RESOURCES

Human beings rely on Earth's resources to survive and build. Some of these resources are renewable, such as wind and sunlight. They can't be used up. Others, such as soil and forests, can be replaced over time. But other resources are **nonrenewable**. That means there is a fixed amount. Nonrenewable sources could someday run out. Nonrenewable resources include **fossil fuels,** such as coal, natural gas, and oil, as well as minerals.

Pumpjacks extract oil from a Kern County, California, oil field.

nonrenewable—not able to be restored or replaced

fossil fuel—natural fuel formed from the remains of plants and animals; coal, oil, and natural gas are fossil fuels

FOSSIL FUELS

Most of the world's energy comes from coal, natural gas, and oil. We process and use these in many different ways. These energy sources power everything from our cars to the furnaces in our homes. But fossil fuels take millions of years to form. Once they are gone, they cannot be replaced. The burning of fossil fuels also causes pollution and damages the environment.

Retrieving fossil fuels can have negative effects as well. Mining often has a lasting impact on the environment. Surface mining involves stripping away the plant life, soil, and rock. Mining also creates huge amounts of waste rock. Sometimes the waste is dumped into old work sites that become empty pits. These pits often fill with water, forming lakes. The poisonous waste of minerals such as copper and uranium sometimes leaks into the soil or ends up in these lakes.

After all natural resources are extracted, an open pit mine is abandoned in Lead, South Dakota.

COAL

Most coal is burned to produce electricity. But it can also be processed into both a liquid and a gas. Coal gas powered the first gas lighting systems more than 200 years ago. Liquid coal can be used as a fuel for vehicles. Another important product from coal is a solid gray substance called coke. It is made by baking coal at high temperatures. Coke is used as a fuel or in the process of making steel.

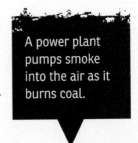

A power plant pumps smoke into the air as it burns coal.

Crude oil is poured from a bucket.

OIL AND NATURAL GAS

Oil, or petroleum, is a thick, black, energy-rich liquid. Petroleum is also sometimes called crude oil. It is a mixture of many substances. To use it, the different materials within crude oil must be separated. Most of the world's oil is used to make fuels. It is also used to make products such as plastics, motor oil, wax, and pavement for roads.

Natural gas occurs naturally in a gas form. It consists mostly of a gas called methane. It also contains propane and butane gases. Natural gas powers furnaces, stoves, and other appliances. Compressed natural gas can be used to power motor vehicles.

Fossil fuels won't last forever. However, the use of renewable sources such as solar energy, geothermal energy, and wind energy are on the rise. All of these sources provide energy while causing less damage to the environment.

FACT

One day, mining companies may have to dig and drill deeper, and under more difficult conditions, to reach fossil fuels. At the rate we now use fossil fuels, some scientists estimate the world's reserves will only last 40 to 70 more years.

CHAPTER 4

ALTERNATIVE ENERGY SOURCES

SOLAR ENERGY

Energy from the sun is called solar power. People collect this power in a number of ways. Solar panels soak up sunlight and convert it into electricity. Solar thermal plants use many large mirrors to focus sunlight onto a small area. This focused sunlight creates tremendous heat. This is then used to turn water into steam that powers electricity-generating **turbines**. The sun's heat can also be used to warm water for homes, businesses, or swimming pools. Water is pumped through pipes in glass panels called solar thermal collectors.

Solar fields are placed in wide open areas that receive a lot of sunlight.

turbine—a machine with blades that can be turned by wind or a moving fluid such as steam or water

Some people put solar panels on their homes or property to save on energy bills.

The best part about solar energy is that sunlight is free. However, solar panels are not. Building solar power stations is very expensive. The main drawback of solar power is that it's not always available. It requires an area that receives a lot of sunlight. Solar plants don't produce at night or when clouds hide the sun. Storing solar energy can also be difficult.

GEOTHERMAL ENERGY

The heat within Earth is a powerful energy source. It is called geothermal energy. The temperature of the earth gets hotter deep underground. The deeper the spot, the hotter it gets. Geothermal power can be collected several ways. One way is by drilling wells into cracks in rocks where the groundwater is hot. The hot water or steam either flows up or is pumped up. It then turns turbines that generate electricity. Another way to use this power is by pumping water down to hot rocks in the earth. The water turns to steam, which comes up through pipes and turns turbines. The turbines then drive electric generators.

diagram of a geothermal power plant

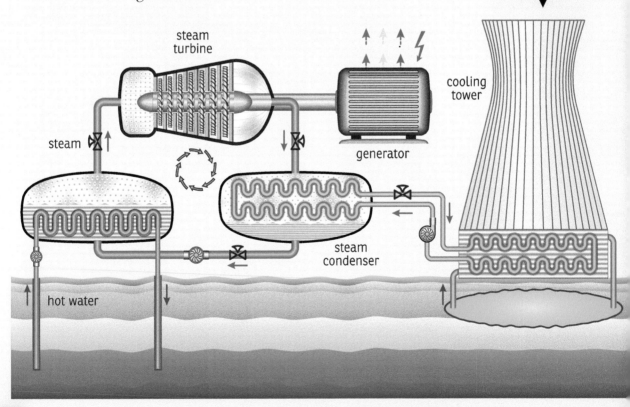

steam turbine

generator

cooling tower

steam

steam condenser

hot water

geothermal power plant in Iceland

FACT

Some homes use geothermal energy for heating. A liquid is pumped through pipes that run deep underground. The liquid is heated and pumped back to the surface. The heat it carries radiates into the building.

WIND ENERGY

Wind is another source of energy. For centuries people have used windmills to harness the energy of wind. Wind pushes the propeller-like blades on these towers. The energy from this motion can be used to pump water, grind grain, or power a generator to produce electricity. Electricity-generating windmills are called wind turbines or wind generators.

Wind power is the fastest-growing energy source in the world. It is free and creates no waste. Wind energy is renewable because wind keeps blowing. But wind is not always reliable. It often works best alongside other energy sources. Some people have criticized wind farms for damaging wildlife, including bats and migratory birds.

a wind turbine farm in the Netherlands

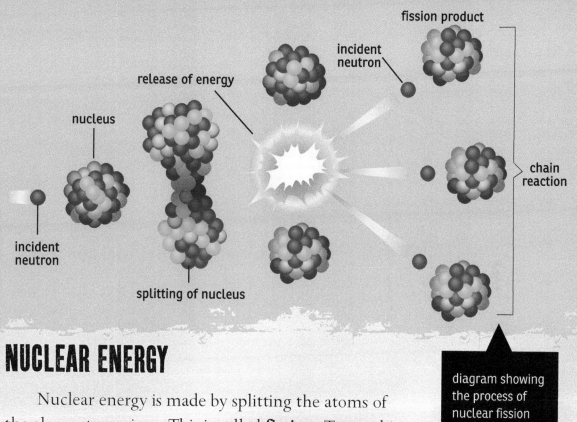

fission product

incident
neutron

release of energy

nucleus

chain
reaction

incident
neutron

splitting of nucleus

diagram showing
the process of
nuclear fission

NUCLEAR ENERGY

Nuclear energy is made by splitting the atoms of the element uranium. This is called **fission**. To get this energy source, workers at nuclear power plants shoot neutrons into uranium atoms. The atoms break apart, releasing energy and more neutrons. Those neutrons hit other atoms, which also break apart. This is called a chain reaction.

Nuclear power makes about 11 percent of the world's energy. It makes a great deal of energy from a very small amount of fuel. Nuclear power costs about the same as coal power, but it generates less air pollution. However, nuclear waste is **radioactive** and very dangerous. It takes special care and handling. The radioactive waste has to be sealed and buried for many centuries before the radioactivity fades.

fission—splitting apart of the nucleus to create large amounts of energy

radioactive—having to do with materials that give off potentially harmful invisible rays or particles

HYDROPOWER

Water power is another renewable resource. In fact, it's the most abundant. Some power is harnessed from flowing water to create electricity. Nearly 10 percent of power plants in the United States run on hydropower.

Water rushes through a dam's turbines to produce electricity.

HOW HYDROPOWER WORKS

Rivers are a natural source of flowing water. The moving water contains huge amounts of kinetic energy, or the energy of motion. Hydroelectric power plants use this energy. The power plants are built across rivers, and the water flows through turbines. The turbines spin and generate electricity.

Tidal Energy

Besides flowing rivers, researchers also experiment with other sources of hydropower. The constant motion of ocean waves is a powerful force. An oscillating water column uses the energy of these rising and falling waves. Shaped like a round chimney, the column lets in ocean waves at the bottom. The waves rise in the chamber. Each time a wave pushes up, the rising wave forces air out of the chamber. The air pushes a turbine that generates electricity.

Tides can also turn turbines. A tidal barrage is a dam that spreads across an inlet — a place where water passes through a narrow channel near land. As the tide comes in, water flows through turbines, generating electricity. Then the water collects in a reservoir behind the barrage. As the tide pulls the water out, the water passes through the turbines again. So a tidal barrage can generate electricity during both high and low tides. Researchers are also developing tidal turbines that would work a lot like wind turbines. Mounted underwater, the turbines would spin as strong tides pass by them.

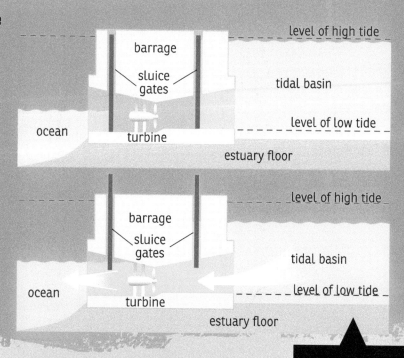

Most hydropower stations rely on dams. They control a river's flow. Dams can create an area of water upstream called a reservoir. The reservoir serves as a large storage of controllable, potential energy. As the dam allows the stored water to flow downhill, pipes or tunnels channel the water to turbines. Then the water exits out the other side of the dam.

Tidal barrages and turbines are powered by ocean waves produced by tides.

HOW CAN HUMANS HELP?

We can all do our part to limit our use of Earth's resources. In the modern world, humans have become more aware of their impact on the environment. A greater effort to reduce our impact on Earth has been seen across the globe.

Picking up trash is one way to help clean up the environment.

PROTECTING AND CONSERVING WATER

Humans have realized that dumping waste of any kind into water destroys that water source. Government agencies in the United States have formed over the last 100 years to control and monitor waste. They build treatment plants, clean wastewater, and prohibit industries and factories from dumping chemicals into rivers and streams. The factories' emissions into the atmosphere are also monitored.

Many cities have tried to reduce the amount of waste that doesn't break down naturally, such as glass and plastics. People are encouraged — and often required — to recycle, reuse, and reduce their usage.

Landfills

Cities have also tried to turn their landfills into power sources. A landfill's methane is useful if it is captured. It can be converted into a power source for electric power plants. One of the landfills used by the city of Los Angeles uses its methane gas to provide electricity to 70,000 homes.

Pollutants dumped into a water source can quickly spread throughout a lake, river, or ocean.

You can also make a difference by conserving water. By reducing water usage, we help preserve groundwater supplies. We also use less energy, which is needed to purify and pump the water into our homes. A few simple practices can make a difference. For example, drink tap water. Bottled water may be convenient, but all that plastic adds up. Make sure your dishwasher is full before you run it. The same goes for your washing machine. Wait for a full load of clothes before you turn it on. Also, use cold water. Most of the time, it cleans just as well as hot water, and using it saves energy. Try not to waste water by overwatering lawns. Water early in the morning or in the evening.

Some people conserve water by using rain barrels. These barrels collect rainwater that falls off houses or other buildings. The collected water can be used to water grass or gardens.

Water from rain barrels can be reused for many things, such as watering gardens.

Hanging laundry outside to dry saves on the energy required to use a dryer.

CONSERVING ENERGY

Humans use a lot of energy. But there are some simple steps we can take to reduce the amount we use. Keep lights off when you're not using them. Close the heating and cooling vents in rooms that you rarely use.

If you can, hang your laundry outside to dry. Also, set your dishwasher to air dry. When you cook on the stove, be sure to use the right size burner for the job. A small pot on a large burner wastes energy. Also, if you have one, use a toaster oven to cook small meals. It uses less energy than a big oven.

These may seem like little things, but they can add up. While there are still many ways that humans can improve their activities, a conscious effort to change our impact on Earth is a good start. By doing our part, we can each help to preserve the future of our natural resources and environment.

TIMELINE

1839 — Edmond Becquerel is the first to discover that sunlight can produce an electric current in a solid material.

1850 — The U.S. Wind Engine Company is established.

1859 — Edwin Drake drills the first rock oil well in Pennsylvania. Petroleum becomes a sought-after fuel source.

1874 — The first known use of the term deforestation — the act or result of cutting down or burning all the trees in an area.

1890 — Steel blades for windmills are invented, making windmills more efficient.

1943 — On July 26, Los Angeles suffers its first big smog due to an increase in cars and industry during WWII (1939–1945).

1956

Solar panels first appear on the market.

1973

The Organization of Arab Petroleum Exporting Countries (OAPEC) puts an embargo on oil exports to the United States and the Netherlands, causing an energy crisis.

1978

The Public Utility Regulatory Policies Act of 1978 is passed. It requires companies to buy a certain amount of electricity from renewable energy sources.

1993

The National Wind Technology Center (NWTC) is built. Its purpose is to be the nation's premier wind energy technology research center.

2008

Lowry Landfill Gas-to-Energy facility becomes operational. The new facility takes waste gas and recycles it into renewable energy.

2014

California becomes the first state to generate more than 5 percent of its annual electricity from solar power.

GLOSSARY

anaerobic (an-uh-ROH-bic)—not using oxygen

atmosphere (AT-muhss-fihr)—the mixture of gases that surrounds Earth

biosphere (BYE-oh-sfeer)—the part of Earth in which life can exist

decompose (dee-kuhm-POHZ)—to rot or decay

fission (FI-shuhn)—splitting apart of the nucleus to create large amounts of energy

fossil fuel (FAH-suhl FYOOL)—natural fuel formed from the remains of plants and animals; coal, oil, and natural gas are fossil fuels

greenhouse gas (GREEN-houss GAS)—gases in a planet's atmosphere that trap heat energy from the sun

hydrosphere (HYE-droh-sfeer)—the part of Earth including bodies of water and water vapor in the atmosphere

natural resource (NACH-ur-ul REE-sorss)—something in nature that is useful to people, such as coal and trees

nonrenewable (non-ri-NOO-uh-buhl)—not able to be restored or replaced

radioactive (ray-dee-oh-AK-tiv)—having to do with materials that give off potentially harmful invisible rays or particles

renewable (ri-NOO-uh-buhl)—restored or replaced by natural processes

turbine (TUR-bine)—a machine with blades that can be turned by wind or a moving fluid such as steam or water

READ MORE

Braun, Eric. *Taking Action to Help the Environment*. Who's Changing the World? Minneapolis: Lerner Publications, 2017.

Morris, Neil. *The Landscape*. The Impact of Environmentalism. Chicago: Heinemann Library, 2013.

Parker, Vic. *Saving the Environment*. Kids Making a Difference. Chicago: Heinemann, 2013.

INTERNET SITES

FactHound offers a safe, fun way to find Internet sites related to this book. All of the sites on FactHound have been researched by our staff.

Here's all you do:

Visit *www.facthound.com*

Type in this code: 9781515771968

Check out projects, games and lots more at
www.capstonekids.com

CRITICAL THINKING QUESTIONS

- Name two alternative energy sources. How do they produce energy for humans to use?

- Coal is a nonrenewable resource. What does nonrenewable mean?

- Take a look at the diagram on page 21. Explain how nuclear fission produces energy.

INDEX